DiVISION

Ann Becker

Crabtree Publishing Company
www.crabtreebooks.com

Author: Ann Becker
Coordinating editor: Chester Fisher
Series editor: Penny Dowdy
Editor: Reagan Miller
Proofreader: Ellen Rodger
Editorial director: Kathy Middleton
Production coordinator: Margaret Amy Salter
Prepress technician: Margaret Amy Salter
Cover design: Samara Parent
Logo design: Samantha Crabtree
Project manager: Kumar Kunal (Q2AMEDIA)
Art direction: Dibakar Acharjee (Q2AMEDIA)
Design: Shruti Aggarwal (Q2AMEDIA)
Photo research: Poloumi Basu (Q2AMEDIA)

Photographs:
Dreamstime: Fesus Robert: p. 19 (top)
Fotolia: Ray Kasprzak; p. 20 (bottom);
    Janet Wall: p. 5
Istockphoto: p. 13; Kelly Cline: p. 20; Eric Gevaert:
    p. 20; Jim Jurica: p. 9; Ezgi Kocahan: p. 1; Nicolesy:
    front cover (center); Giacomo Nodari: p. 7; Olaru
    Radian-Alexandru: p. 17; Tony Tremblay: p. 9, 21
Q2AMedia Art Bank: p. 4–5, 6–7, 9, 10–11, 13,
    14–15, 17, 21
Shutterstock: Tereza Dvorak: p. 10–11; Dawn
    Hudson: p. 8; Fedorov Oleksiy: front cover
    (bottom right); Claudia Van Dijk: p. 19 (bottom);
    Elena Show: folio image

Library and Archives Canada Cataloguing in Publication

Becker, Ann, 1965-
    Division / Ann Becker.

(My path to math)
Includes index.
ISBN 978-0-7787-4346-0 (bound).--ISBN 978-0-7787-4364-4 (pbk.)

    1. Division--Juvenile literature. I. Title. II. Series: My path to math

QA115.B424 2009   j513.2'14   C2009-903578-2

Library of Congress Cataloging-in-Publication Data

Becker, Ann, 1965-
    Division / Ann Becker.
        p. cm. -- (My path to math)
    Includes index.
    ISBN 978-0-7787-4346-0 (reinforced lib. bdg. : alk. paper)
    -- ISBN 978-0-7787-4364-4 (pbk. : alk. paper)
    I. Title. II. Series.

    QA115.B428 2010
    513.2'14--dc22

                                    2009022913

Crabtree Publishing Company

www.crabtreebooks.com   1-800-387-7650

Published in Canada
Crabtree Publishing
616 Welland Ave.
St. Catharines, ON
L2M 5V6

Published in the United States
Crabtree Publishing
PMB16A
350 Fifth Ave., Suite 3308
New York, NY 10118

Published in the United Kingdom
Crabtree Publishing
Lorna House, Suite 3.03, Lorna Road
Hove, East Sussex, UK
BN3 3EL

Published in Australia
Crabtree Publishing
386 Mt. Alexander Rd.
Ascot Vale (Melbourne)
VIC 3032

Contents

Let's Have Fun!

Charlie and his stepdad arrive at school. He has waited all week. Today is the school carnival!

Charlie looks at the map. He wants to visit every booth. The map looks like an **array**. Charlie says it looks like a multiplication problem. His stepdad says it looks like a **division** problem, too. Division means splitting something into **equal groups**.

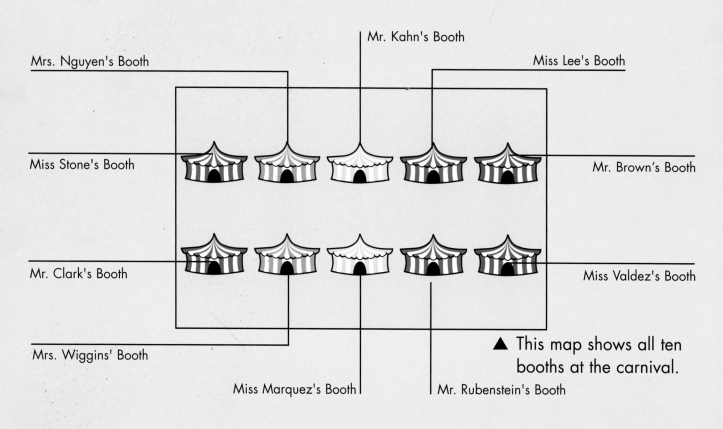

Mr. Kahn's Booth

Mrs. Nguyen's Booth

Miss Lee's Booth

Miss Stone's Booth

Mr. Brown's Booth

Mr. Clark's Booth

Miss Valdez's Booth

Mrs. Wiggins' Booth

▲ This map shows all ten booths at the carnival.

Miss Marquez's Booth

Mr. Rubenstein's Booth

Charlie and his stepdad visit the school carnival.

Fact Box

The word *division* has many meanings. Every kind of division describes groups of things.

Equal Groups

Charlie's stepdad looks at the map. He shows Charlie that the booths are in 5 groups.

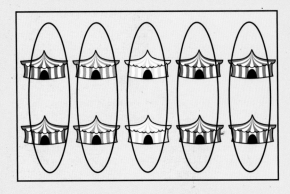

◀ The booths are in 5 groups.

All of the groups have 2 booths.

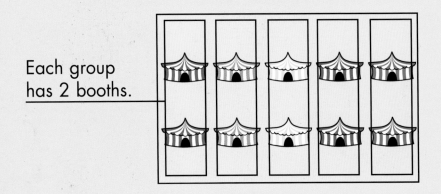

Each group has 2 booths.

Since all of the groups have the same number, Charlie can call them equal groups. Charlie now knows that 10 can be divided into 5 equal groups of 2.

Charlie and his stepdad look at the map.

Welcome to the Maple Public School Carnival

More Arrays

Charlie's stepdad buys tickets for the carnival. He shows Charlie that the group of tickets makes up an array. Charlie looks at the array and smiles. "I know we have 12 tickets because the array shows 3 groups of 4 tickets. I know 3 times 4 is 12," Charlie says proudly.

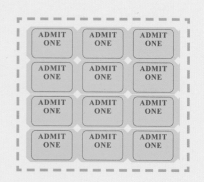

"Exactly," says Charlie's stepdad. "Did you know that you can use your multiplication facts to solve division problems? They are opposites." Charlie's stepdad shows him what he means.

$3 \times 4 = 12$

$12 \div 3 = 4$

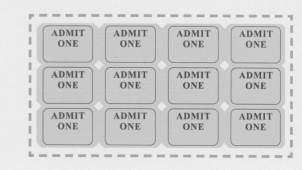

Fact Box

A **division sign** looks like this: ÷

Charlie's stepdad buys tickets for Charlie.

A **fact family** shows all the related multiplication and division facts for a set of numbers. This is the fact family for the numbers 4, 5, and 20.

$4 \times 5 = 20$

$5 \times 4 = 20$

$20 \div 5 = 4$

$20 \div 4 = 5$

A fact family is usually made up of two multiplication questions and two division questions.

Dividing by 2

Charlie wants to try dividing. He looks at the first booth. This is what he sees at the ring toss booth.

Charlie sees that the array has 12 bottles. The bottles are in 2 groups. Charlie counts the bottles in the two groups. He counts 6 bottles in each group. So he writes:

$12 \div 2 = 6$

Activity Box

Imagine putting one more bottle in each of the two groups. What would the division problem be?

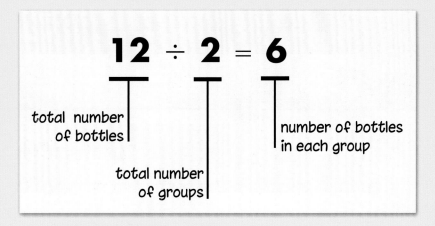

$$12 \div 2 = 6$$

total number of bottles

total number of groups

number of bottles in each group

Charlie walks to the side of the booth.
Now the array looks like this:

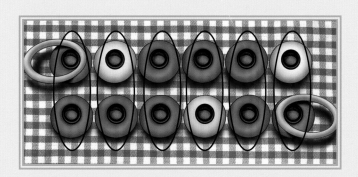

◀ Turning the array changes the groups and the number of bottles in each group.

Charlie sees that the array has 6 groups.
So he writes:

$$12 \div 6 = 2$$

total number of bottles

total number of groups

number of bottles in each group

Dividing by 5

Charlie learns he can use **repeated subtraction** to solve any division problem. His stepdad shows him how.

Charlie's stepdad gives him a group of 20 balloons. He asks Charlie to use repeated subtraction to divide the 20 balloons by 5. Charlie knows this means he needs to subtract, or take away, 5 balloons from the 20 balloons as many times as he can.

Fact Box

You can divide any number that ends in 0 or 5 by the number 5.

$20 - 5 = 15$
$15 - 5 = 10$
$10 - 5 = 5$
$5 - 5 = 0$

How many subtraction problems did Charlie do? Four. So $20 \div 5 = 4$.

Charlie's stepdad shows Charlie a number line. It can show repeated subtraction, too.

14   15   16   17   18   19   20   21   22   23   24   25

▲ Each hop on the number line is subtracting 5.

The number line shows you can subtract 5 from 20 a total of 4 times.

Dividing by 3

Charlie took a while to learn to multiply by 3. Will it take him a long time to learn to divide by 3? Charlie knows two ways to divide now. He will divide both ways.

The next carnival booth has 18 rubber ducks in the water. How many groups can Charlie make if each group has 3 ducks?

Charlie imagines the ducks in an array first.

He can find the answer by dividing 18 ducks into 3 groups. Charlie solves the division problem. The answer is 6. He can make 6 groups with 3 ducks in each group.

Charlie tries the division problem again. This time he uses a number line to show repeated subtraction. Charlie starts at 18 and subtracts by 3. He can subtract 6 times. Charlie knows that $18 \div 3 = 6$.

▲ Each hop on the number line is subtracting by 3. There are 6 hops. So, $18 \div 3 = 6$.

Division Words

Charlie's stepdad explains that each **operation** has special words. Division has words for all three numbers in the problem.

$$14 \div 2 = 7$$

dividend

divisor

quotient

Charlie understands. The **dividend** is the number that is divided into groups. The **divisor** is the number to divide by. The **quotient** is the answer to the division problem.

Activity Box

Remember that each fact family usually has two multiplication sentences and two division sentences. Find the fourth sentence to complete the fact family:

$5 \times 6 = 30$ $6 \times 5 = 30$ $30 \div 6 = 5$

Charlie's stepdad writes a division problem. He asks Charlie to write the correct division words on the three numbers of the problem.

$$10 \div 5 = 2$$

dividend

divisor

quotient

Charlie knows words that tell about division.

Division Rules

Charlie's stepdad says division problems are easier to solve when you know the rules. He gives Charlie a paper listing these rules.

Rule 1: Any number divided by 1 is the same number.

$9 \div 1 = 9$ $17 \div 1 = 17$ $100 \div 1 = 100$

Rule 2: A number divided by itself always equals 1.

$7 \div 7 = 1$ $33 \div 33 = 1$ $400 \div 400 = 1$

Rule 3: The number 0 divided by a number always equals 0.

$0 \div 4 = 0$ $0 \div 58 = 0$ $0 \div 900 = 0$

Rule 4: You cannot divide by 0. It does not make sense. You cannot break something into groups of 0.

◄ $6 \div 1 = 6$
Six bears divided into one group means six bears in one group.

◄ $3 \div 3 = 1$
Three toys divided into three groups means one toy in each group.

◄ $0 \div 9 = 0$
When you divide 0 toys into 9 groups, each group has 0 toys!

◄ Do not divide by 0. You cannot make 0 groups!

Dividing is Easy!

Charlie likes division. His stepdad gives him two problems to try. Get a piece of paper and divide with Charlie!
What is 20 ÷ 5?

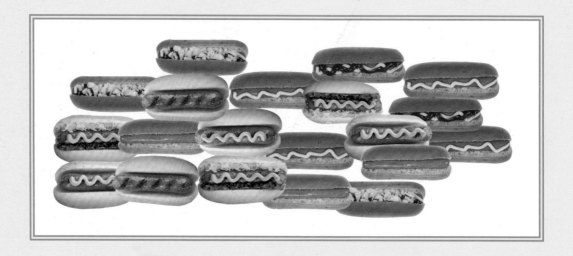

What is 16 divided by 2?

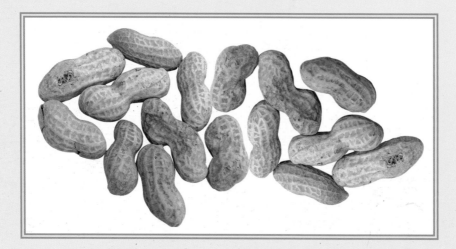

Dividing is almost as much fun as the carnival!

Glossary

array A group of objects in rows and columns

dividend The number that is divided into groups

division Numbers split into equal groups

division sign ÷

divisor The number to divide by

equal groups Groups with the same amount of items

fact family Related facts, such as $3 \times 4 = 12$, $4 \times 3 = 12$, $12 \div 3 = 4$, and $12 \div 4 = 3$

operation Addition, subtraction, multiplication, or division

quotient The answer to a division problem

repeated subtraction Subtracting by the same number many times

You can use this division chart to help you learn your division facts.

DIVISION

÷	1	2	3	4	5	6	7	8	9	10
1	1	2	3	4	5	6	7	8	9	10
2	2	4	6	8	10	12	14	16	18	20
3	3	6	9	12	15	18	21	24	27	30
4	4	8	12	16	20	24	28	32	36	40
5	5	10	15	20	25	30	35	40	45	50
6	6	12	18	24	30	36	42	48	54	60
7	7	14	21	28	35	42	49	56	63	70
8	8	16	24	32	40	48	56	64	72	80
9	9	18	27	36	45	54	63	72	81	90
10	10	20	30	40	50	60	70	80	90	100

Look in the division chart for the number 20. This is the dividend. Look above the 20 for the number 5. This is the divisor. The number 4 on the left is the quotient. It can also be written as $20 \div 5 = 4$.

Index

Printed in the U.S.A. — BG